P9-CER-834

DAYS OF CHANGE

Creative Education

BY VALERIE BODDEN

Published by Creative Education
P.O. Box 227, Mankato, Minnesota 56002
Creative Education is an imprint of The Creative Company.

Cover design and art direction by Rita Marshall
Interior design and book production by The Design Lab
Printed in the United States of America

Photographs by Alamy (Scott Camazine, Chad Ehlers), Corbis (Bettmann, Chase Swift, Hulton-Deutsch Collection, Minnesota Historical Society), Getty Images (AFP, Keystone / Stringer, National Archives, Time Life Pictures)



Library of Congress Cataloging-in-Publication Data
Bodden, Valerie.
The Bombing of Hiroshima and Nagasaki / by Valerie Bodden.
p. cm. – (Days of change)
Includes bibliographical references and index.
ISBN-13: 978-1-58431-545-0
1. Hiroshima-shi (Japan)—History—Bombardment, 1945—Juvenile literature. 2. Nagasaki-shi (Japan)—History—Bombardment, 1945—Juvenile literature. I. Title.
D767.25.H6B63 2007
940.54'2521954–dc22 2006019824

9 8 7 6 5 4 3

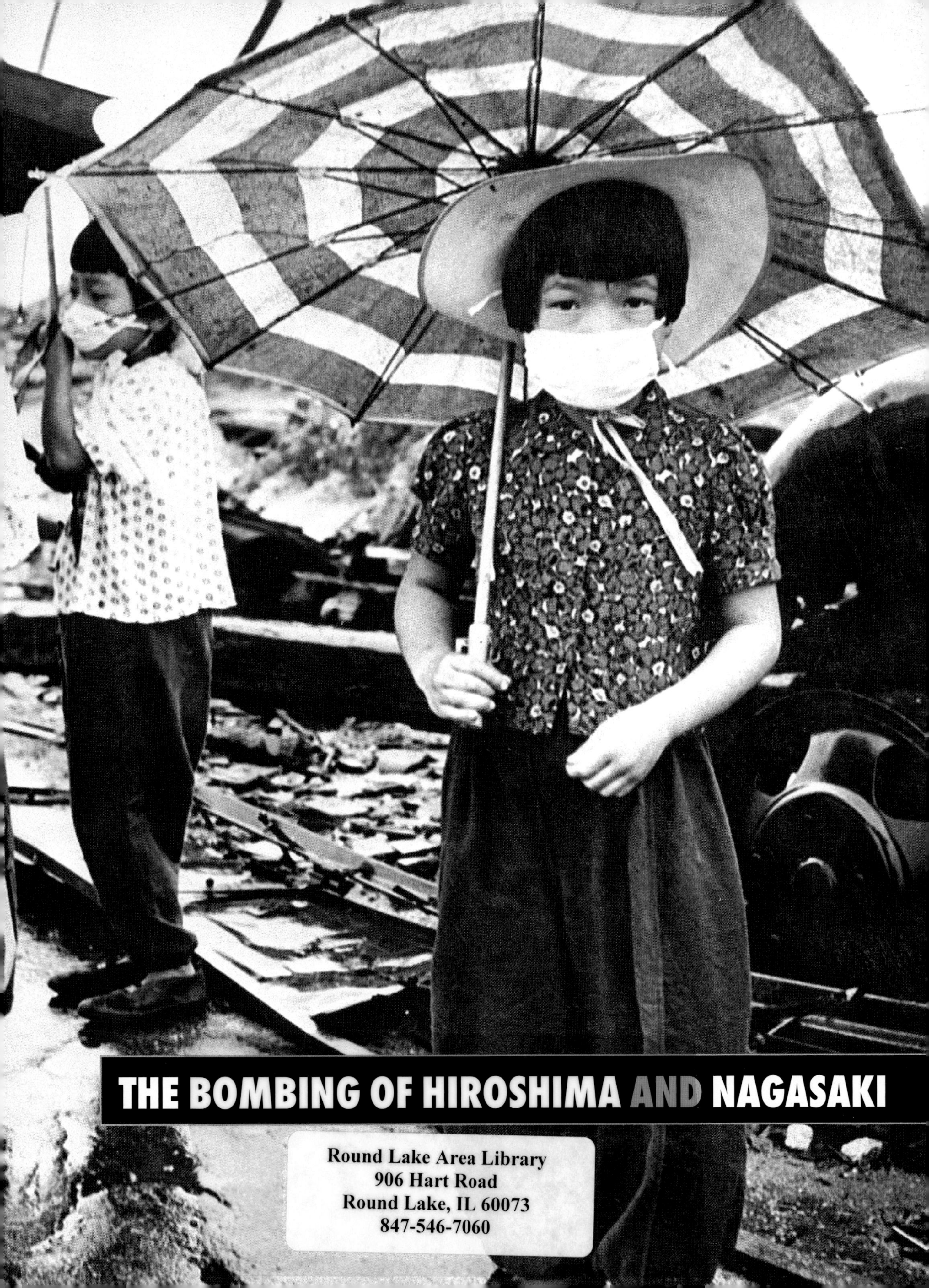

# THE BOMBING OF HIROSHIMA AND NAGASAKI

Within the mushroom clouds that towered over Hiroshima and Nagasaki (above) after t
atomic bombs exploded, debris was tainted with radiation before falling back to Earth

A mushroom-shaped cloud of smoke churned and boiled over the city of Hiroshima, Japan, growing and bubbling until it reached more than nine miles (14.5 km) into the sky. Inside the B-29 bomber *Enola Gay*, flying rapidly away from Hiroshima, American airmen peered at the debris strewn below, watching as raging fires sprang up across the city, soon blazing so fiercely that the smoke blocked the devastation from sight. As the plane left the city—but not images of its destruction—behind, the *Enola Gay*'s copilot wrote in his logbook, "My God, what have we done?"

What they had done was drop a new kind of weapon—an atomic bomb—destroying with one plane and one bomb what had previously required hundreds of planes carrying thousands of tons of bombs. Only days later, another American plane would drop an atomic bomb on the city of Nagasaki, 200 miles (320 km) away, and the Japanese would surrender, bringing World War II to a close. At the same time, a nuclear arms race would begin, along with more than 60 years of debate about the use of atomic weapons, a debate in which the people of Hiroshima and Nagasaki would serve as dramatic reminders of the horrifying toll exacted by such weapons.

## TOTAL WAR

The use of the atomic bomb on Hiroshima came at a time when the world was battle-weary and war-torn. Six years earlier, in 1939, German troops under the direction of dictator Adolf Hitler had invaded Poland, sparking World War II, which soon became a brutal, bloody conflict involving nearly every nation on Earth. As the war progressed, huge numbers of casualties mounted as both sides embraced the idea of "total war," in which both soldiers and civilians were at equal risk of enemy fire. As countries abandoned previous rules of warfare that had set civilians off-limits as targets, people thousands of miles behind the front lines had to fear for their lives, and air raid drills became common in Washington, D.C., London, and other cities throughout the world.

Although the United States had at first tried to keep its troops out of the war, the country was drawn into the conflict when Japan bombed the American naval base at Pearl Harbor, Hawaii, in a sneak attack on December 7, 1941, killing more than 2,400 American sailors. Immediately, the country mobilized for war, and the nation's men headed overseas to fight in both the Pacific and Europe (where Germany and Italy had declared war on the U.S.). At home, women stepped into the workforce en masse, with more than six million taking jobs that had traditionally been held by men, from driving garbage trucks to felling trees. Many found themselves employed in the nation's war industry, riveting, welding, and assembling airplanes and weapons.

With their attack on Pearl Harbor, the Japanese hoped to disable America's Pacific naval fleet so that the U.S. would be unable to interfere in Japan's planned takeover of the colonies of Southeast Asia. The Japanese presumed that the shock of such an attack would force the U.S. to surrender quickly. Rather than leading to a quick peace, however, the attack on Pearl Harbor spurred the Americans to war. Later reports of Japan's brutal treatment of prisoners of war only added more fuel to Americans' hatred for Japan. A 1944 poll revealed that one in eight U.S. residents believed that everyone in Japan should be killed after the war.

More than 1,000 men went down with the USS *Arizona*, one of 21 U.S. naval vessels sunk or destroyed in the Japanese attack on Pearl Harbor.

Despite the fact that no battles were ever fought on the American home front, Americans were reminded of the war on a daily basis. With many goods in short supply and needed by the military, Americans at home dealt with the rationing of items from ketchup and meat to shoes and gasoline. Nearly everyone on the home front was involved in one form or another in promoting American victory, from planting Victory Gardens (private gardens intended to help relieve the burden on the public food supply) to knitting socks for soldiers overseas.

> *"[The atomic bomb has been used] against those who attacked us without warning at Pearl Harbor, against those who have starved and beaten and executed American prisoners of war, against those who have abandoned all pretense of obeying international laws of warfare. We have used it in order to shorten the agony of war, in order to save the lives of thousands and thousands of young Americans."*
>
> HARRY TRUMAN,
> U.S. president, August 9, 1945

Meanwhile, in the countries of South America, the effects of the war were also felt, although they were largely positive, as South Americans supplying rubber and other materials for the U.S. war effort received a better price for their goods than they had in the past. In the countries of northern Africa, as well, the war had some advantages. Although fighting extended into several North African nations and caused localized damage, some countries, such as Egypt and Libya, benefited from the construction of new transportation facilities, including airports.

In Europe, it was a different story entirely, as civilians here became the first victims of the new total war. Cities from London, England, to Warsaw, Poland, were destroyed

Spurred on by patriotic posters, World War II-era Americans planted Victory Gardens, producing a third of the vegetables consumed in the country in 1943.

In the fall of 1940, an average of 200 German planes bombed London every night, severely damaging much of the city, including the beautiful St. Paul's Cathedral.

by bombs released from German aircraft, and the German cities of Dresden and Hamburg were reduced to ashes by British and American bombers, killing thousands of civilians. Countless more suffered at the hands of Hitler's Nazis (National Socialists), who wanted to establish a "pure" Germanic race and forced Jews and others into ghettos and concentration camps, where 11 million were killed.

In the Soviet Union, as well, civilians fared poorly throughout most of the war. As the Germans took over part of the Soviet Union during the early years of the war, they slaughtered massive numbers of people. The ensuing bitter battles between the Soviets and the Germans—such as that at Stalingrad (modern Volgograd)—caused much destruction to the landscape. Despite the devastation brought to

From September 1940 to May 1941, German bombs destroyed more than a million houses in the United Kingdom, leaving many families and children homeless.

their country by the Germans, the Soviets were eventually able to turn the tide, pushing the Nazis back to Berlin and helping to bring about a German surrender in May 1945.

Yet, even as victory celebrations broke out across Europe, war continued to rage between Japan and the allied nations of the U.S., Britain, China, and Australia. Although the Japanese had enjoyed early victories, taking over Malaya, the Philippines, Hong Kong, Singapore, and Burma, by 1942, the Americans and their allies had begun to drive them back across the Pacific toward Japan. Even as they faced devastating defeats, however, Japanese soldiers continued to fight valiantly for their nation, inflicting heavy casualties on American forces, as the Japanese—who saw surrender as dishonorable—almost always fought to the death. They also began to stage kamikaze, or suicide, attacks, flying airplanes or piloting boats directly into enemy targets.

Japanese kamikaze pilot

Everyday life in Japan had become a struggle for its citizens, who faced severe shortages of food, fuel, and medical supplies. But until 1945, the people were largely spared from the direct effects of the war. Then, just

Although kamikaze pilots were sometimes shot down before reaching their targ
ikazes were responsible for sinking 34 U.S. ships and killing 4,900 U.S. sai

*"Somebody opened my door and shouted, 'Hiroshima has been destroyed!'; about 100,000 people were thought to have been killed. I remember the feeling of unease, indeed nausea, when I saw how many of my friends were rushing . . . to celebrate. Of course they were exalted by the success of their work, but it seemed rather ghoulish to celebrate the sudden death of 100,000 people, even if they were 'enemies.'"*

Otto Frisch, Manhattan Project scientist, 1979

Emperor Hirohito of Japan

after midnight on March 10, 1945, more than 300 American aircraft dropped 2,000 tons (1,800 t) of incendiary bombs—which spread a thick gasoline-jelly mixture that ignited raging fires—on the Japanese capital of Tokyo, killing nearly 100,000 people. Over the course of the next few months, nearly every major city in Japan was damaged in American bombing raids (launched from U.S. bases in the Mariana Islands), which eventually killed nearly a million people. Despite the devastation to their homeland and the fear of more attacks, most Japanese citizens were unwavering in their loyalty to their leader, Emperor Hirohito, whom they regarded as a god.

As the bombing campaigns and American battle victories continued, it became clear to many officials both within and outside of Japan that the country had no chance of defeating the U.S. Yet most Japanese authorities continued to resist the unconditional surrender that the U.S. called for, as they feared it would mean the removal of Emperor Hirohito from the throne. Instead, the Japanese prepared for a final, massive battle, ordering all men ages 15 to 60 and all women ages 17 to 40 to help with the effort. The government provided civilians with spears and sharpened tools and taught them how to strap explosives



The firestorm unleashed by the incendiary bombs dropped on Tokyo destroyed 15 square miles (39 sq km) of the city, leaving a million people homeless.

to their bodies and hurl themselves at American tanks. They were prepared to fight the enemy down to the last person.

Meanwhile, in the U.S., a fight to the last person was the last thing most citizens wanted. Yet, believing that the war in the Pacific would continue for at least another year, Americans steeled themselves for more casualty reports from a war that had already cost 50 million lives, about 400,000 of them American. The U.S. government developed a plan for a large-scale Japanese invasion, called "Operation Downfall," but leaders secretly hoped to never have to put the plan into action, as they were also working on a new weapon that had the potential to bring the war to a swift close.

In 1939, German-born physicist Albert Einstein—who had moved to the U.S. because of the Nazi persecution of Jews in Germany—had written a letter to President Franklin Roosevelt, warning that the Germans had successfully split an atom of the element uranium, a breakthrough that could potentially lead to the development of incredibly powerful atomic bombs. As a result, Roosevelt set up a committee to investigate the potential of nuclear power. Once the U.S. entered the war, research into an atomic bomb became more urgent, and

*"Atomic [fission]—which is without a doubt the greatest discovery in the history of the world—puts in the hands of men an instrument of prodigious power. Applied to peaceful ends, it can liberate men from menial or exhausting tasks, guarantee them every comfort, . . . and dispel, for all men, the worries about tomorrow, giving them a smiling future. Applied to destructive ends, it is capable of spreading across the Earth a desolation of which the imagination cannot conceive. We are today at the crossing of two paths: here is the happiness of men; there are the worst calamities."*

M.A. Fouillé, French professor of physics, 1945

In 1945, the world's first atomic bomb was test-detonated from a 100-foot-high (30.5 m) steel tower; after the test, the tower was gone, melted by the explosion.

Not all Manhattan Project scientists supported the use of the atomic bomb in a surprise attack against a Japanese city. Some felt that the Japanese should be warned about the bomb before it was dropped. Others suggested dropping the bomb in a remote area of Japan to show its destructive power while sparing lives. The first option was rejected by U.S. officials because many felt that a warning would give Japan the opportunity to shoot down the plane carrying the bomb. The second option was also rejected, as some feared that if a demonstration bomb failed to explode, the Japanese would be encouraged to continue fighting.

The July 1945 test bomb was so powerful that people 10 miles (16 km) away felt its heat, and residents 300 miles (480 km) away reported seeing a brilliant flash of light.

the president established the Manhattan Project, gathering many of the world's brightest scientists at a top-secret, high-security base at Los Alamos, New Mexico, with the mission of developing the world's first atomic bomb before either Germany or Japan—which both also established atomic bomb programs—could.

*"We waited until the blast [of the 1945 test bomb] had passed, walked out of the shelter, and then it was extremely solemn. We knew the world would not be the same. A few people laughed, a few people cried. Most people were silent. I remembered the line from the Hindu scripture, the* Bhagavad-Gita*: . . . 'Now I am become death, the destroyer of worlds.' I suppose we all thought that, one way or another."*

ROBERT OPPENHEIMER, Manhattan Project scientific director, 1965

Under the direction of scientist Robert Oppenheimer and U.S. Army Brigadier General Leslie Groves, work on the bomb went forward at lightning speed. Four years—and $2 billion—later, in July 1945, the world's first atomic bomb was tested successfully in the New Mexican desert, and the U.S., under President Harry Truman (who had taken office following the death of Roosevelt on April 12), was ready to use it to bring an end to the war in the Pacific.



At the height of the Manhattan Project, Robert Oppenheimer (third from left) and the other scientists at Los Alamos worked 18 hours a day, 6 days a week.

# THE *PIKADON*

At 7:09 A.M. on the morning of Monday, August 6, 1945, the air raid siren blared in Hiroshima, interrupting the morning routines of the coastal city's 300,000 or so residents, who were busy preparing breakfast and heading for work. Many hurried to their neighborhood bomb shelters. Twenty-two minutes later, Hiroshimans breathed a collective sigh of relief as they heard the all-clear signal. A false alarm, most believed. With as much vigor as they could muster in the sweltering heat and stifling humidity, the city's citizens returned to the various tasks that had become commonplace since the beginning of the war. Some walked or biked through the streets and across one of the city's seven rivers to jobs in Hiroshima's war industries. Soldiers exercised on the city's parade grounds. Schoolgirls and other volunteers worked to create firebreaks to protect their city from the bombing that many believed was inevitable. In fact, as they worked, many in Hiroshima wondered once again why their city had so far been spared the destructive bombing raids that so many other Japanese cities had endured.

Suddenly, Hiroshimans looked up to see three American B-29 bombers flying high above the city. Most were unconcerned. The types of firebombings that had ravaged other Japanese cities required hundreds of bombers carrying thousands of tons of bombs. These three bombers posed little threat, the citizens thought. Few noticed the large, shiny object that had been dropped from one of the planes and was speeding toward the ground, falling nearly 6 miles (10 km) in 43 seconds.

The advent of the atomic bomb was made possible by the 1938 discovery—by German scientists Otto Hahn and Fritz Strassmann—that the atoms of certain elements, including uranium, could be split through a process known as nuclear fission. When atoms are split, miniscule particles called neutrons are expelled from them with incredible force. In an atomic bomb, the expelled neutrons smash into other atoms in their path, causing the process to start all over again, with more and more atoms simultaneously splitting and expelling neutrons that, in turn, split other atoms. As the atoms split, huge amounts of energy in the form of heat and radiation are released.

Before the atomic bomb was dropped on Hiroshima, it was a bustling city—the seventh-largest in Japan—and the headquarters of the country's Second General Army.

Then, with a sudden, blinding flash, the object—the 9,000-pound (4,100 kg) "Little Boy" atomic bomb—exploded 1,900 feet (580 m) above the Shima Surgical Hospital, sending a huge fireball roaring outward. A violent shockwave shook the area, and an enormous mushroom-shaped cloud billowed up over the city, causing nearly total darkness where moments before had been the brightest light imaginable. As those who had survived the mysterious *pikadon* (Japanese for "flash-boom") picked themselves up from the ground and looked around, they were met by a scene unlike any they had ever witnessed before: nearly every building in the city had been completely flattened, dead bodies covered the ground, and survivors, looking almost otherworldly, stared at the ruins of their city in confusion.

Twenty-five-year-old Hiroshiman surgeon Terufumi Sasaki had just drawn blood from one of his patients at the Red Cross Hospital and was headed toward the facility's laboratory when the atomic bomb exploded. After the shockwave had passed, Dr. Sasaki found the hospital in complete chaos. The patient whose room he had just come from was dead, as was a colleague in the lab he had been headed for. In fact, Dr. Sasaki was the only uninjured doctor in the hospital, and he spent the next three days working nearly nonstop—with only one hour of sleep—to treat the 10,000 patients who flooded the 600-bed hospital.

Hiroshima was chosen as the target of the first atomic bomb in part because its terrain was almost entirely flat, which meant the bomb's blast would have maximum effect.

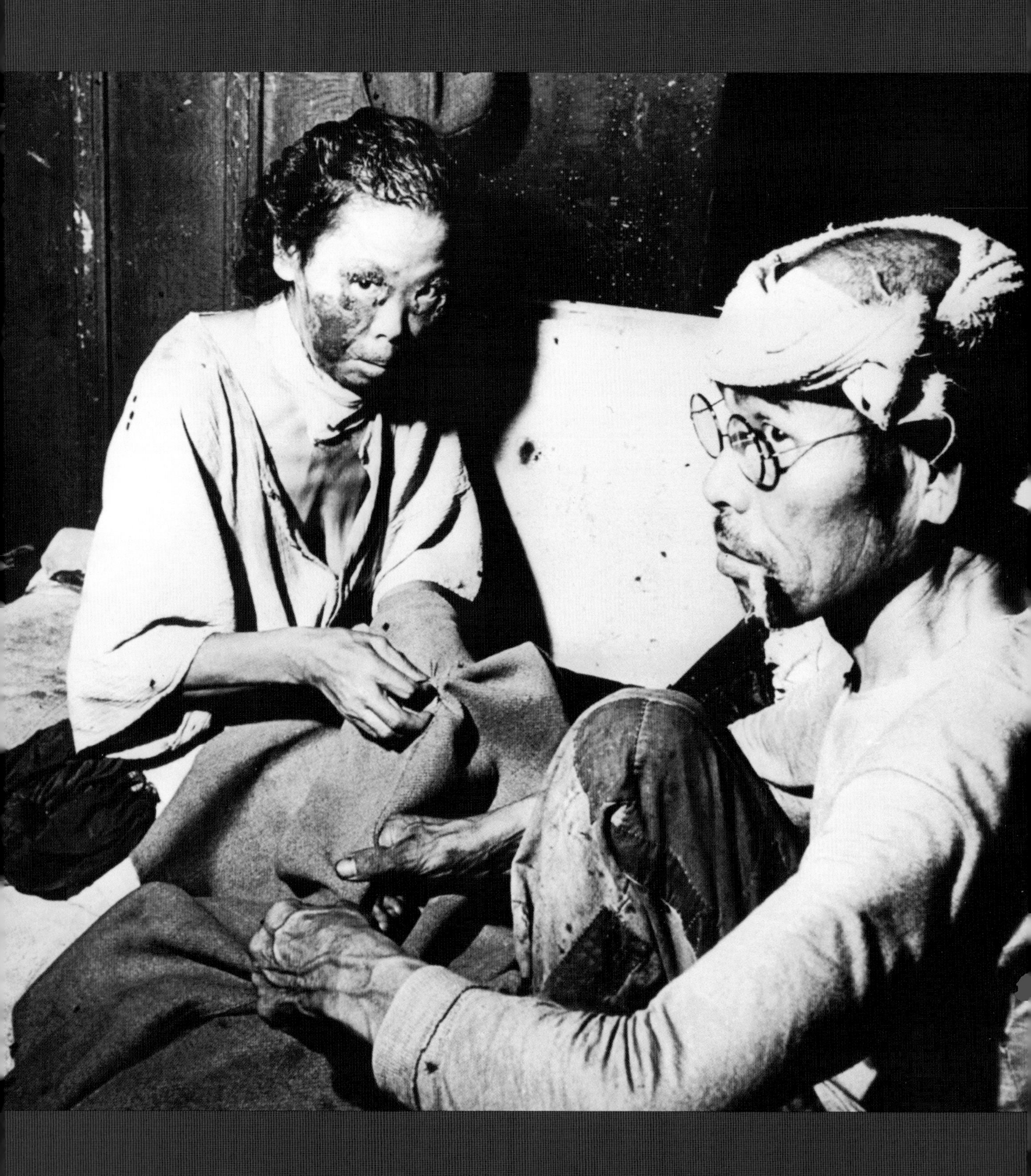

People up to two miles (3.2 km) from Hiroshima at the time of the bomb blast suffered severe burns; in many cases, the outer layer of skin was completely destroyed.

Most didn't yet realize that thousands of Hiroshimans were simply gone, vaporized by the intense heat of the flash—which had raised temperatures on the ground to 5,400 °F (3,000 °C). All that remained of them were ashes—and sometimes a shadow that had been seared into the ground by the brilliant flash. Even people farther from the hypocenter had been killed instantly, although their bodies remained, lying burned and disfigured on the ground. Others had died when the bomb's shockwave had blown apart buildings, sending houses and debris flying and crushing people under layers of rubble. In all, an estimated 70,000 people who had been alive mere seconds before were now dead.

*"The appearance of people was . . . well, they all had skin blackened by burns. . . . They held their arms bent [forward], . . . and their skin—not only on their hands, but on their faces and bodies too—hung down. . . . If there had been only one or two such people, . . . perhaps I would not have had such a strong impression. But wherever I walked I met these people. . . . Many of them died along the road—I can still picture them in my mind—like walking ghosts."*

SURVIVOR OF THE HIROSHIMA BOMBING, 1962

For those yet alive, the picture was grim. More than 100,000 were injured, many of them suffering from severe burns caused by both the heat and the scorching flash of light. Most were unrecognizable: their skin hung from their hands and faces, their hair had been burned off, and their clothes were missing.

After rounding up what remained of their families, the survivors began to shuffle slowly through the streets, their arms outstretched and slightly bent in order to prevent the burned skin from rubbing. Fires sprang up all around them, sparked by the heat of the bomb, and by cook fires that had been burning in many people's kitchens when the houses had fallen down around them. Powerful winds created by the explosion fanned the flames, and the fires quickly engulfed the debris.

Those who were trapped in rubble called out for help, but, as the fires closed in, most survivors were able to assist only their relatives and close neighbors, leaving those who were unable to help themselves to die in the flames. As they sought to escape the hellish inferno, thousands jumped into the city's rivers, with many drowning. Others made their way to Asano Park on the Kyo River, one of the few parts of the city that hadn't yet been touched by fire. About 40 minutes after the bomb exploded, a cold rain began to fall,

After the fires burned out in Hiroshima, survivors had little hope of recovering any of their belongings; most found only charred ruins where their homes had once stood.

*"A shattering flash filled the sky. I was thrown to the ground and the world collapsed around me. . . . I couldn't see anything. It was completely dark. . . . When I finally struggled free, there was a terrible smell, and I rubbed my mouth with a towel I carried around my waist. All the skin came off my face, and then all the skin on my arms and hands fell off."*

Futaba Kitayama, survivor of the Hiroshima bombing, 1985

but rather than providing refreshing relief, the rain was black and sticky, filled with radioactive particles, and more than a few people feared that it was oil dropped by American planes to feed the flames.

Survivors flocked to the three hospitals in the city that had survived the blast. Yet, with 90 percent of Hiroshima's doctors dead or wounded, the hospitals could do little for their patients aside from bandaging cuts and putting compresses of saline solution on the worst burns. In each hospital, the injured soon filled the beds, the floors, the stairways, the bathrooms, the courtyards, and the streets outside. Because most of the injured suffered from diarrhea and vomiting—effects of the massive doses of radiation they had received when the bomb exploded—and were too weak to move, the hospitals were soon covered with filth. By the afternoon, medical personnel and military relief parties from other areas of Japan began to trickle into the city, but for the most part, the people of Hiroshima were on their own.

Those who were well enough to move searched through the bodies and rubble of the city for lost relatives and friends. Others began to cremate the dead. Most noticed that the city had become eerily quiet. While some of the worst wounded cried out occasionally for water, others lay on the ground in silent agony. That night, the people of Hiroshima slept wherever they



In addition to the thousands of Japanese victims of the atomic bomb, many prisoners of war, such as these Javanese men, were also injured or killed.

The "Fat Man" atomic bomb that fell on the shipbuilding city of Nagasaki was originally destined for the city of Kokura, 95 miles (150 km) to the north. When the American B-29 carrying the bomb arrived over Kokura, however, the city was obscured by heavy cloud cover, so the pilot turned the plane toward his secondary target: Nagasaki. Weather conditions almost prevented the dropping of the bomb there, too, but at the last minute, the bomb was released through a hole in the clouds, missing its target—the Mitsubishi Shipyards—by one and a half miles (2.5 km) and exploding above the Urakami Cathedral, Japan's largest Roman Catholic church.

Like the bomb dropped on Nagasaki, postwar Fat Man bombs—named for their bulky shape—weighed 10,000 pounds (4,500 kg) and measured 5 feet (1.5 m) in diameter.

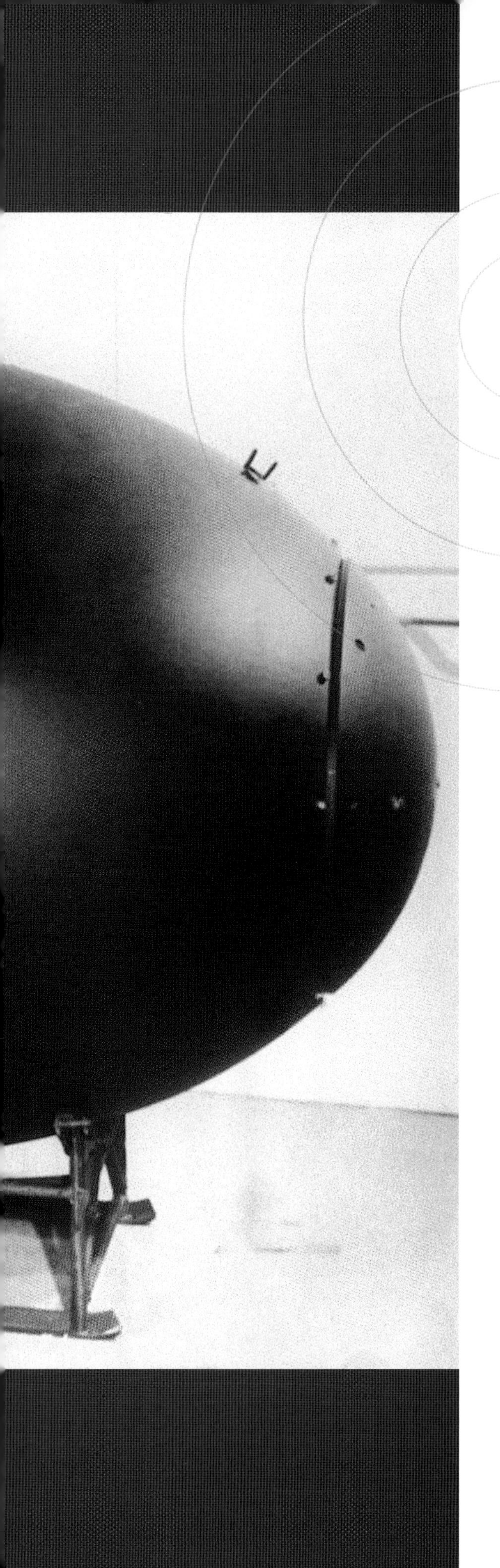

could find a place to lie down. Many never got up the next morning.

Meanwhile, in the Japanese capital of Tokyo, officials who had learned of the bomb argued over whether or not the country should surrender. Shortly after the attack on Hiroshima, the U.S. had issued a press release stating that the bomb dropped on the city had been atomic. America warned that if the Japanese did not accept the U.S. terms of surrender, they could expect "a rain of ruin from the air, the like of which has never been seen on this Earth."

Three days later, on August 9, having received no response from the Japanese government, the U.S. unleashed that rain of ruin on the port city of Nagasaki, once a favorite destination of American and British travelers. The bomb dropped on Nagasaki, nicknamed Fat Man, was a plutonium device, more powerful than the uranium Little Boy bomb dropped on Hiroshima. Yet, thanks to the hills that surround the city of Nagasaki, its effects weren't as devastating as Little Boy's had been. Still, more than a third of the city's buildings were razed to the ground, and 40,000 people were killed instantly in temperatures that caused birds to combust in mid-flight, iron to melt, and telephone poles to burst into flame. As in Hiroshima, fires spread through the city, and greasy, radioactive rain fell on survivors.

That same day, the Soviet Union invaded Japanese-held Manchuria in China. Yet, even after learning of the second bombing and the Soviet attack, which had killed 80,000 Japanese soldiers, some within the Japanese government refused to admit defeat, insisting that there was still a way out. Others contended that the time had come for Japan to spare its people from more ruin. Finally, with those in favor of surrender and those opposed to it at a stalemate, Emperor Hirohito was called upon to make the decision. At 2:00 A.M. on August 10, he told his government that it was time to "bear the unbearable." Japan would finally surrender.

*"The war situation has developed not necessarily to Japan's advantage. . . . Moreover, the enemy has begun to employ a new and most cruel bomb, the power of which to do damage is indeed incalculable, taking the toll of many innocent lives. . . . We have resolved to pave the way for a grand peace for all generations."*

EMPEROR HIROHITO,
Japanese ruler,
August 15, 1945

News of Japan's surrender was read with joy by American servicemen, most of whom had been expecting continued battles with high casualty levels.

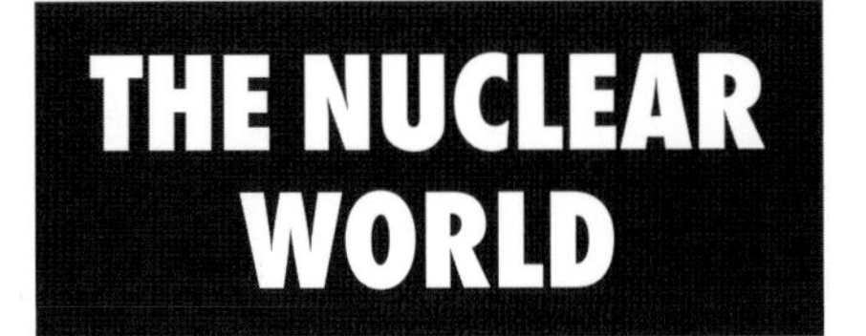


On August 15, 1945, people throughout Japan listened to their radios in disbelief as Emperor Hirohito announced the nation's surrender. As the people of the war-torn country, who had never before heard their emperor speak, learned of Japan's defeat, many wept. Even in Hiroshima, people who had believed that their country would never surrender were shocked by the news—more shocked, according to some survivors, than they had been by the use of the atomic bomb on their city.

Throughout Japan, however, people were grateful that Emperor Hirohito had been allowed to maintain his title, even as a seven-year U.S. military occupation of the country began. Under the occupation government, a massive reconstruction program was quickly set in motion throughout the country, although little special attention was given to the cities of Hiroshima and Nagasaki. In fact, reports of the atomic bombings and their aftereffects were censored by occupation authorities, who didn't want to "disturb public tranquility."

Yet, had journalists been allowed to write about the effects of the atomic bombs, they could have said much about conditions in Hiroshima and Nagasaki, where, two weeks after the bombs were dropped, survivors were falling ill and dying in large numbers. Even those who had seemed to be in good health suddenly displayed a whole host of symptoms, including vomiting, diarrhea, hair loss, red or purple spots on the skin, and bleeding gums. Physicians soon

Even Japanese prisoners of war being held in the Philippines were stunned and dismayed at the news that their homeland had surrendered to the U.S.

In the years after the atomic bombs were dropped, some bomb victims felt it was their responsibility to bring the plight of survivors to the world's attention. Kiyoshi Kikkawa, a guard at the Hiroshima Electric Company, suffered terrible burns on his back during the bombing, and as they healed, grotesque scars called keloids formed. After the war, Kiyoshi opened a souvenir shop and would bare his back for any who wanted to see his scars. Although he was accused by some of "selling the bomb," Kiyoshi felt that it was his duty to show the world what this terrible new weapon had done.

Life in Hiroshima and Nagasaki after the bombs was especially difficult for children, thousands of whom lost their parents and were left as orphans.

figured out what was ailing these bomb survivors: radiation sickness, caused by the colossal amounts of radiation—x-rays, gamma rays, beta particles, and neutrons—that had been released by the bombs. Although some recovered, by the end of 1945, 200,000 people who had been in Hiroshima or Nagasaki during the bomb blasts were dead.

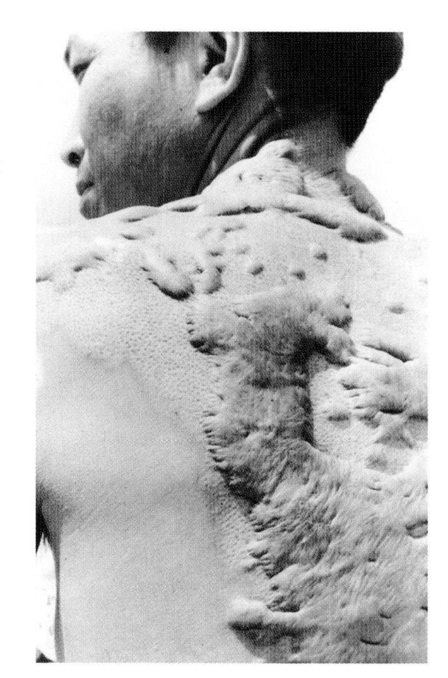

Keloids on a bomb victim's back

Even for those who lived through the bombs and the threats of radiation sickness, conditions were terrible. A lack of food and medicine continued to plague Hiroshima throughout the fall and winter of 1945, and many survivors lived on a diet of dumplings made of horseweed grass and ground acorns. With nearly 98 percent of the city's buildings destroyed or severely damaged, people lived in makeshift shelters created from the rubble, but these did little to keep the winter cold out. The situation was little better in Nagasaki, where housing needs were also desperate.

Yet, even amid such dreadful conditions, there were signs of hope. By the beginning of September 1945, wildflowers were already springing up among the ruins, putting an end to speculation that nothing would grow in the bombed cities for decades. Rumors that the cities would be uninhabitable by humans for 75 years were also squelched after scientists measured radiation levels in Hiroshima in September and announced that people could live there safely. Bolstered by such reports, rebuilding efforts were soon in full swing in Hiroshima and Nagasaki, and by 1955, the populations of both cities surpassed the 1945 levels.

Even with their cities rebuilt, however, survivors—who came to be known as *hibakusha*, Japanese for "explosion-affected people"—continued to suffer in the years after the bombs. Many were permanently disfigured by keloids—masses of thick, copper-colored scar tissue produced by the serious burns they had received. They also experienced higher than normal rates of many types of cancer, most notably leukemia. Many who had been children at the time of the bombing experienced stunted growth, and babies

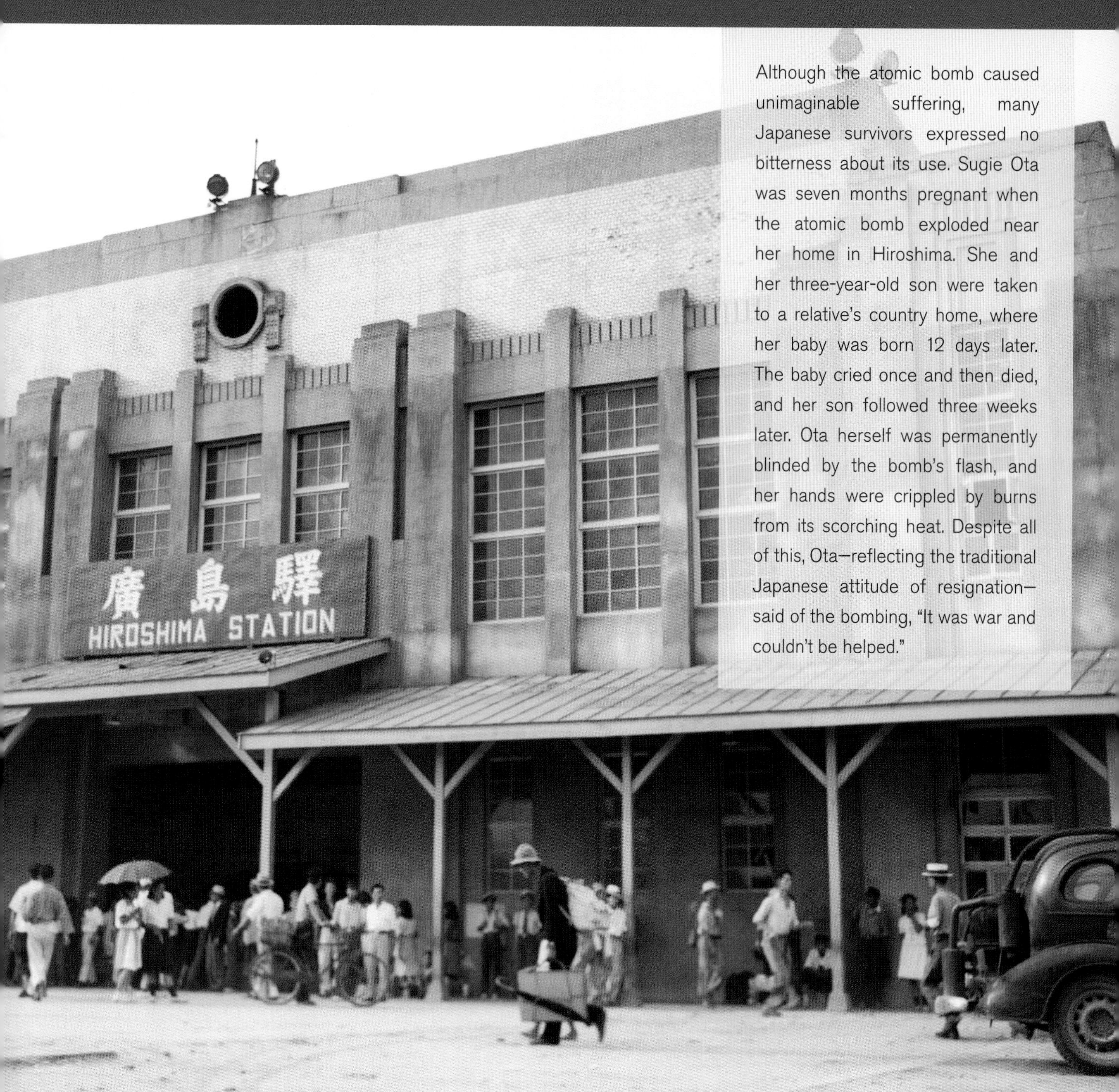


Although the atomic bomb caused unimaginable suffering, many Japanese survivors expressed no bitterness about its use. Sugie Ota was seven months pregnant when the atomic bomb exploded near her home in Hiroshima. She and her three-year-old son were taken to a relative's country home, where her baby was born 12 days later. The baby cried once and then died, and her son followed three weeks later. Ota herself was permanently blinded by the bomb's flash, and her hands were crippled by burns from its scorching heat. Despite all of this, Ota—reflecting the traditional Japanese attitude of resignation—said of the bombing, "It was war and couldn't be helped."

Hiroshima's need for transportation led the city's railroad station to be one of the first buildings to be rebuilt after the bombing, with reconstruction completed by July 1946.

In 1955, 11-year-old Sadako Sasaki, who had been 2 when the bomb was dropped on Hiroshima, was diagnosed with leukemia. Her friends told her that if she folded 1,000 paper cranes, the gods would make her well. So Sasaki began to fold. On October 25, 1955, Sasaki died, and 1,000 of the paper cranes she had folded were placed in her coffin with her. Inspired by Sasaki's courage, her classmates began a peace movement that resulted in the Children's Monument—a life-sized statue of Sasaki holding a paper crane—at Hiroshima's Peace Memorial Park. Today, thousands of paper cranes from around the world surround the monument.

Those who send paper cranes to the Children's Monument add their voices to the plea beneath the statue: "This is our cry, this is our prayer: peace in the world."

who were in their mothers' wombs when the bombs exploded were often born with abnormally small heads and suffered from mental retardation. In addition to their physical complaints, many *hibakusha* faced discrimination and were shunned by employers, who had learned that bomb victims were prone to a variety of ailments, including severe fatigue.

It wasn't only the people of Hiroshima and Nagasaki whose lives changed when the first atomic bombs were dropped, however. In those moments, life changed for the people of the entire world. The introduction of nuclear weapons into modern warfare meant that, for the first time, the population of an entire city could be virtually wiped out with a single weapon. Yet, although many were frightened by the new power that had been discovered, most in postwar America supported President Truman's use of the bombs on Hiroshima and Nagasaki, which they saw as necessary to bring an end to a brutal war. In France, many books and newspapers celebrated the dawn of the "atomic age" and the leap in science that it represented. Even in Japan, many accepted the fate that had befallen them, noting that it was war, and such things happened in war.

*"I took no pride or pleasure then, nor do I take any now, in the brutality of war, whether suffered by my people or those of another nation. Every life is precious. But I felt no remorse or guilt that I had bombed the city where I stood. . . . My crew and I had flown to Nagasaki to end the war, not to inflict suffering. There was no sense of joy among us as we walked the streets there [less than a month after the bombing]. We were relieved it was over, for us and for them."*

CHARLES SWEENY, pilot of the plane that dropped the bomb on Nagasaki, 1997

Others weren't so sure that the use of the atomic bomb had been justified. Some, including General Dwight Eisenhower, the supreme commander of the Allied forces in Europe (and future president of the U.S.), felt that the Japanese had already been near the point of surrender and that the bombs were unnecessary. Others suggested that if the U.S. had offered to allow Emperor Hirohito to retain his title from the beginning, Japan may have surrendered sooner. Some calculated that predictions that half a million American soldiers would have been lost had the planned invasion of Japan gone forward were wildly inflated. Still others argued that the U.S. had dropped the bomb not so much to end the war as to show the Soviet Union, a rising world power, its full might. In many nations, including U.S. ally England, people began to call for international control of this awesome new form of power.



Before such control could be established, however, a nuclear arms race erupted between the U.S. and the Soviet Union, which had entered a period of tension known as the Cold War almost immediately after the end of World War II. In 1949, the Soviet Union tested its first atomic bomb, while the U.S. continued to churn out its own bombs, with more than 200 in its arsenal by 1949. As tensions between the two countries increased during the 1950s and '60s, both continued to create more and more powerful weapons capable of being launched from half a world away. By the 1980s, there were 50,000 nuclear warheads in the world; together, they were capable of creating an explosive force equaling more than one and a

With the threat of impending nuclear war during the 1950s and '60s, American schoolchildren practiced covering their heads and taking shelter in hallways.

*"In this last great action of the Second World War, we were given the final proof that war is death. War in the 20th century has grown steadily more barbarous, more destructive, more debased in all its aspects. Now, with the release of atomic energy, man's ability to destroy himself is very nearly complete. The bombs dropped on Hiroshima and Nagasaki ended a war. They also made it wholly clear that we must never have another war. This is the lesson men and leaders everywhere must learn, and I believe that when they learn it they will find a way to lasting peace."*

Henry Stimson, U.S. secretary of war at the time of the bombings, 1947

half million times that of the bomb dropped on Hiroshima. Although many of these bombs have since been dismantled under the authority of various treaties, nuclear weapons are today held by at least 7 countries, with an estimated total of 30,000 weapons among them—more than enough to destroy the world.

This, say the people of Hiroshima and Nagasaki, can never be allowed to happen. Today, Hiroshima has adopted the mission of fostering peace in the world; it now calls itself the "City of Peace" and annually hosts an international conference against the use of nuclear weapons. Although the City of Peace has been rebuilt into a modern city of towering skyscrapers, elegant hotels, and designer stores, reminders of the city that once lay in ruins abound. The most striking is the burned-out shell of the former Industrial Promotion Hall, now known as the A-Bomb Dome. Preserved as a symbol of the destruction wrought by the atomic bomb, this building, once a center of activity in Hiroshima, now stands in Peace Memorial Park, where more than 70 monuments commemorate *ayamachi*, "the mistake."

*"I recovered six months later, but my neck remained stuck to my left shoulder and three fingers of my right hand were fused together. . . . Because of my disfigured face, people often threw stones at me and mocked me, saying, 'A monster is coming!' . . . My scars finally got better, and I applied for jobs, but I was always turned down: 'We can't hire you because of your face.' . . . It took three years of treatment [in the U.S.] for my neck to return to its original position and each finger to separate from the others. My face had 37 operations."*

YAMAOKA MICHIKO, survivor of the Hiroshima bombing, 1984

Doves—released as a symbol of peace—fly near the empty skeleton of the A-Bomb Dome each year on the anniversary of the bombing of Hiroshima.

In the mid-1950s, 25 women who had been severely disfigured by the bombing of Hiroshima were flown to New York, where doctors at Mount Sinai Hospital operated on them free of charge. Known as the Hiroshima Maidens, the women stayed with Quaker families between surgeries in which they had keloids removed, new eyebrows tattooed on, and skin grafted over their burns. Although one Maiden died under anesthesia, the project continued, with surgeons performing a total of 127 operations on the women. The operations didn't completely heal the Maidens' scars, but they did give the women a renewed sense of confidence, enabling them to go out in public again.

Brightly colored lanterns floating calmly on Hiroshima's Motoyasu River serve as a silent but powerful reminder of the lives devastated by the atomic bomb.

Each year on August 6, the people of Hiroshima gather at Peace Memorial Park to reflect on the events of that fateful August morning in 1945. In the evening, they light paper lanterns decorated with the names of relatives who died as a result of the bombing and set them afloat on the city's rivers. Their hope is that the memory of their suffering will prevent the nations of the world from ever again resorting to nuclear warfare. So far, it has.

# BIBLIOGRAPHY

Chisholm, Anne. *Faces of Hiroshima*. London: Jonathan Cape, 1985.

Grant, R. G. *Hiroshima and Nagasaki*. Austin, Tex.: Raintree Steck-Vaughn, 1998.

Hersey, John. *Hiroshima*. New York: Scholastic, 1985.

Lawton, Clive A. *Hiroshima: The Story of the First Atom Bomb*. Cambridge, Mass.: Candlewick Press, 2004.

Lifton, Betty Jean. *A Place Called Hiroshima*. New York: Kodansha International, 1985.

Weinberg, Gerhard. *A World at Arms*. Cambridge: Cambridge University Press, 1994.

Ziff, John. *The Bombing of Hiroshima*. Philadelphia: Chelsea House Publishers, 2001.

# INDEX